THE INVOLVED PARENT'S SEVENTH-GRADE GUIDE

BY
ELLEN SHRAGER

Illustrated by Abby Bosley and Anthony T. Shelton, Sr.

TEACHER VOICE PUBLISHING
P.O. BOX 446
VILLANOVA, PA 19085

For information about special discounts for bulk purchases, please contact Teacher Voice Publishing at 1-610-355-0553- or teachervoicepublishing@comcast.net

Illustrated by Anthony T. Shelton, Sr. and Abby Bosley

MANUFACTURED IN
THE UNITED STATES OF AMERICA

Library of Congress Control Number: 2010930237

ISBN 978-0-9793200-0-2

To

all the parents out there who want to do the right thing
and listen to the village, but just need some
encouragement to do it; may this be that encouragement.

and to Anne, Dee, George, John, and Mary for sharing
their children with me.

CONTENTS

INTRODUCTION

Technology has forever changed parenting.

Previous generations of parents* would turn to their own parents for advice on how to navigate the choppy waters of raising adolescents. But today's grandparents have no experience to share on how to handle cyber-bullying, how to appropriately respond to grades posted online, how to appropriately limit texting, or how to undo an adolescent mistake forever embedded on the Internet.

Today's involved parents are on their own and understandably fearful that one misstep may cause permanent damage or at the very least be the cause for their child not obtaining a coveted college acceptance. These parents create a "trophy student" and evaluate their parenting skills based on the quality of their child's college acceptances.

They are short-sighted for two reasons.

First, the retention rate of college freshmen returning as sophomores to the same four-year institution is reported to be approximately 76% in the United States: one in four students don't return!

Second, these "trophy students" are now perceived as high-maintenance employees in the workforce. These

---

*As a literary device, I use "parent" and "parents" to include guardians and family members other than parents raising our students.

employees are unable to independently meet deadlines without their managers' reminders.

To use a football metaphor, these short-sighted parents mistakenly stopped at the 20 yard-goal and congratulated themselves on a job well done without realizing the next twenty yards would determine the quality of their child's *adult* life.

These misguided parents are afraid of what will happen to their children if they don't get accepted to the "right" college when they should be afraid of what will happen if their children can't be honest with them or can't accept natural consequences.

By focusing merely on the college acceptance, in my opinion, many of today's involved parents overshoot their role of "protective manager" to their elementary school children and fail to make the timely transition to their role of "coach" to their adolescents.

By the time the parents realize what they should have been doing, they have missed the grace period when grades and consequences do not impact college applications and teacher evaluations: seventh grade.

Seventh grade is the perfect time to let your child make mistakes. This willingness to let your child falter will go against your instinct to help create success, but will pay dividends in your child's future: scoring well on the Teacher Evaluation for college applications, staying in college, and keeping a job upon graduation.

How do I know?

I used to work in the admissions office at Boston College. Later, I taught high school and, as the class advisor, became privy to how scholarships, letters of recommendations and awards are bestowed on our seniors. Currently I teach seventh grade in a large junior high building of seventh, eighth and ninth graders.

Over the course of my teaching career, I have taught over 3,000 adolescents. I keep in contact with and follow many of my former students. I am privy to a lot that goes on with them and with my own large extended family and friends.

The insight gained from these relationships and from my own teaching experience is shared in my book, *Teacher Dialogues*. From Wenatchee, Washington, to Portland, Maine, I train teachers to guide parents to truly help their children.

As I visit different schools for teacher training, I require an advance list of the biggest employers in the area and the parents' list of desirable colleges. I contact the college, and based on my prior work experience in the admissions office and my assurance that I have no child trying to gain admission, I ask key questions and receive frank answers from the admissions counselors. I also contact the human resource office at the largest employers and do the same. I share this information with teachers so that they can help parents.

Now, I am sharing it directly with parents because many parents are crafting their child's experiences based on parental fears and illusions rather than today's college admission reality. Why do today's parents do this?

Societal Changes Influence Parenting

Society has changed since I first started teaching and these parental reactions are a logical consequence of these societal changes. In my opinion, the top three changes in society that result in parental fear are:

1. With more options for women, many couples delayed starting a family and had difficulty creating a family. Growing up as a baby boomer, my friends and I frequently acquired unplanned siblings; in contrast, my brother-in-law views the odds of his daughter's birth taking place as one in a million. Parents with fewer children may be more protective than parents with more children.

2. The media stokes parental fears and paranoia about child safety, creating a society of obsessive observers who watch their children over the Internet, on the nanny cam, and even when the child is away at camp or overseas. Once the child leaves elementary school and the opportunity for parental involvement in the building disappears, some parents struggle

with having a child out of their reach during the day. The events of 9/11 have heightened our sense of vulnerability in this country, making parents understandably more fearful.

3. High-stakes testing and job outsourcing stoke the fear of increased competition, compelling some parents to emphasize grades, not learning. They are concerned that the glut of people with college degrees means that many college graduates will not find jobs with the benefit of health insurance. My parents believed that as long as we went to college and got a good liberal arts education, we would be able to provide for ourselves. Today's parents believe that if their child doesn't go to the right college and the right grad school, they will never find a job and never match the lifestyle in which they were raised.

Perhaps because both parents work and spend only a few hours a day with their child, they are motivated to make those few hours be pleasant and conflict-free.

My father also felt that time with his loved ones was very precious. He was drafted into WWII at the age of 27 and didn't start a family until later in life. He described parenthood as cutting out your own heart and putting it in the careless hand of a toddler who can easily, unintentionally break it. He would say that once you have children your day can only be as good as one of your children's worst moments.

In spite of my father's tenderness for us, he would never understand today's TV shows depicting children running the house and parents afraid and unwilling to correct them.

My father believed that correcting children is an act of love and a sacred obligation; the parent-child bond would be strengthened, not diminished, by correction. This is in stark contrast to my colleague, who also became a father later in life. He told me that he doesn't believe in time-outs or consequences for his sons because it hurts too much. In spite of being a seventh-grade teacher for 25 years, he just can't do it.

"KIDS Rule"

While historically parents have always feared losing their child to death, some of today's parents have so much vested in so few children that they carry the burden of an additional fear: some parents fear losing their child's companionship more than they fear losing their jobs or divorcing.

Consequently, they won't enforce consequences because they are terrified that their child's temporary frustrations and anger at being held accountable will result in rejection.

Some parents fear ultimately losing their child's approval. This thought is so devastating to them, that when their children do make mistakes, *and it is impossible for adolescents not to make mistakes*, these parents refuse to believe the truth. Instead, they spin illusions to justify the disconnect with reality. They deprive their child of converting a mistake into a learning experience and the results will be disappointingly obvious when it comes time to fill out college applications and teacher evaluations.

Our Beloved Children

When did you know in your heart that you wanted to become a parent?

I frequently ask people this question. Among my circle of friends and family, it frequently happens after the birth of someone else's baby, or after attending a four-year-old's ballet recital, or after an amazing conversation with someone's tyke.

I have yet to hear "Well, I was shopping in the mall and saw a bunch of thirteen-year-olds hanging out and after noticing the way they dressed, wore makeup, and the tone of voice they used with one another, I said to myself hot dang, I need to get me one of those."

There is one caveat. While we teachers recognize that some of the students are physically maturing at younger ages, we all have noticed a solid small group of students who are "late-bloomers" for a variety of reasons, e.g., the increasing number of "preemies" or the increasing number of students on the spectrum. When I speak of seventh graders, I am excluding that 10% that have a history of developmental delay.

I have taught every grade from seventh to the second year of college and seventh grade is my favorite; I love to teach seventh grade . . . right up until February!

Adolescent Behavior

What happens in February when most of my students have turned thirteen?

I don't know if it is hormones, becoming a teenager, or something else, but there is a definite shift to seeking more approval from peers than from parents or teachers.

I warn parents that they will not recognize some of the behaviors that their child will most likely demonstrate. One parent compared it to an alien intermittently taking over their precious child's mind with no warning and no set schedule.

- ♥ Independent thinkers suddenly put their own sense of right or wrong in their backpack and care more about what others think.

- ♥ A natural talent for soccer will suddenly switch to another sport if it is "the" sport for other students!

- ♥ A student who comes home and tells you everything about her day deftly omits some events that you only discover from other sources.

- ♥ A pacifist will suddenly haunt you until you buy the violent video game that all of his friends are playing.

- ♥ A student's life-long friendship will be ditched overnight to enhance his or her own status with "cooler" students.

- ♥ Students will seek out their own identity with clothing, hairstyles, body image, and start becoming interested in the opposite sex.

Most parents understand these examples; at this point you may be nodding your head in agreement at the classic adolescent behavior that comes with the territory.

But, then I also mention some behaviors that surprise parents so much that the head nodding stops. Most parents are stunned by the list that I have culled from thousands of teachers from all fifty states and Canada attending my presentations.

These teachers want parents to know:

- ♥ This is the year your child may manipulate adults against one another, whether it be parent against teacher, parent against parent, grandparent against parent.

- ♥ This is the year your child may omit parts of the truth as a passive lie to you.

- ♥ This is the year your previously honest child may directly lie to you.

- ♥ This is the year your previously honest child may be caught cheating on a quiz or test.

- ♥ This is the year your child may submit a project that is pure plagiarism off the Internet.

- ♥ This is the year your previously compliant child may openly defy authority.

- ♥ This is the year that your child may avoid consequences by using excuses like "I didn't know" or "That teacher doesn't like me."

- ♥ This is the year your previously kind child does something unrecognizably cruel to another child, even a former good friend.

- ♥ This is the year parents fully realize the extent that Facebook, texting, e-mail, and video games distract students from studying.

- ♥ This is the year your child may act out problems and deviant behavior with electronic technology, such as cyber-bullying for girls and porn fascination for boys.

- ♥ This is the year your child may deeply disappoint you.

Most first-time parents to an adolescent are shocked by this list. Perhaps you are too. Typically, most parents begin to process this list by thinking about their child's friends and neighbors and can begin to picture specific children doing a few of these things.

Most parents believe in their heart that it won't be their child, just someone else's child. As one mother explained to me, "Our son began to speak at nine months. He has always been so verbal that we thought that we would just talk him through adolescence without having to go through it—boy, were we wrong!"

It is better for your child to try out these undesirable behaviors during seventh grade, and for you to process these occurrences with them. Viewed through the lens that this is typical behavior and not a reflection of your parenting, you can correct your child so that the behavior is addressed and disappears before ninth grade. Why is ninth grade so important?

The Importance of Ninth Grade

Day one of ninth grade is when the school starts tracking your child's class rank compared to all of the other students in his or her class. It is considered a better indicator to college admissions of how your child performs during this age of alleged grade inflation.

Also, students applying for colleges during the beginning of their senior year forward the transcript from ninth to eleventh in their preliminary application. You do not want grades in ninth and tenth grade reflecting your child's poor study habits, habits that should have been learned in seventh and eighth grade.

Your child will be asking the high school teachers for letters of recommendation, preferably from a teacher who has known your child for a few years and not just the first few months of senior year. You do not want these teachers correcting the behaviors that should have been corrected in seventh grade but were ignored because the parents weren't ready to deal with them.

Perhaps one of the biggest differences between when you applied to college and when your child applies to college is that approximately 400 colleges use the Common Application. Your child fills out one application, the teacher fills out one evaluation, and it is sent to as many colleges as you want or can afford. With the one application and early decision being a popular choice among seniors, there is little time to apply, learn from your mistakes, adjust, and apply somewhere else.

For the rest of this book we will:

- ♥ Relate seventh grade behaviors to the Common Application.

- ♥ Discuss how to talk to your adolescent when these behaviors arise in such a way that you get to the heart of the matter.

- ♥ Examine some of the habits your child should be acquiring.

- ♥ Review when to manage, when to coach, and how to train your seventh grader to appropriately negotiate with teachers.

SEVENTH-GRADE BEHAVIORS

AND

THE COMMON APPLICATION

Parents and teachers shouldn't be judged on the presence or absence of problems, but on how they respond to them.

INTEGRITY

The book, *Internet Era: a Wake-Up Call* by Ann Lathrop and Kathleen Foss cites these statistics:

- ♥ 80% of high school students admit to cheating.

- ♥ 95% of students who cheat say they don't get caught.

- ♥ 34% say their parents never talk to them about cheating.

The statistic that approximately one-third of parents never talk to students about cheating corresponds with my experience.

One parent, a fellow teacher married to another teacher, told me in disbelief, "We asked our son why he had the cheat sheet out for your quiz and he said, 'Because you told me if I wanted to play baseball I had to get good grades no matter what!' We told him *'that didn't mean cheating,'* and he replied 'you never said that.' Can you believe this? He is the son of two teachers—we never thought we had to spell this out to him!"

Another mom told me, when I saw her daughter take a student's homework out of his backpack and start copying unbeknownst to the student who had done the work, "Mrs. Shrager, I just don't recognize that as being one of my daughter's behavior because her father and I never taught her to do that!"

When told that your child cheated on a test, or copied someone else's homework, your first instinct will be, "There are two sides to every story, what is my child's side?" While that is true between elementary school equals, that is not true between teacher and adolescent student.

We are not equals. With adolescence, there is reality as observed by the teacher and an adolescent trying to avoid a consequence for a bad choice or an impulsive action. By inviting the child to be equal to the teacher you are setting your child up to lie to you and to cling to that lie.

This is dangerous—your child needs to learn that he or she will survive your being informed of their adolescent mistakes and that both you and he or she will quickly get past it.

Otherwise, when there is a big mistake, like he or she is about to get into a car with someone drinking, or isn't about to graduate, *he or she may make a fatal choice because of the lack of practice of telling you disappointing news and lack of learning that you both will survive it.*

Two girls cheated on a quiz in my class.

They both admitted that "Kate" had asked "Jen" for two answers and that "Jen" had supplied them. I told them that this was a disappointment and that both would receive a zero for their quiz grade. Fortunately, it was a quiz and not a test, because I drop the lowest quiz grade at the end of the marking period. However, during interims, their grades would be lowered. If it had been a test, I wouldn't have been able to drop the lowest grade.

In order for me to drop that as the lowest grade, I require that within two days they bring me a note from their parents that they were aware of the cheating incident.

Jen's dad answered back that he was amazed that this had happened. He and his daughter discussed why she couldn't say "no" to her friend even when she knew it was wrong.

She and her dad had a difficult, but great heart-to-heart talk about peer pressure. She offered to send me an apology note as well, and her dad was proud of that. A month later, another student in the class was caught cheating and I heard "Jen" tell him, "Go ahead —do what she says, it is so much better once your parents know."

"Kate's" mom could not hear the truth. She wrote me back that I was mistaken, that her child wouldn't do that, that they were just chatting during the quiz, forgetting that they couldn't talk.

The parent and child could not get to a point of honesty. The daughter learned that her mother couldn't handle the truth, and she was deprived of sharing that her belonging to so many sports teams outside school prevented her from studying. A few months later she was ineligible to play sports because of her low grades in other classes.

From this experience, I learned to listen to a parent's language: when a parent is shrouded in illusion, rather than grounded in reality, the parent refers to "my child" and not to the student by name. It indicates that the parent is unwilling to see the child as a good, albeit imperfect, individual.   Rather, the parent is marketing a "my child" package as a scorecard of his or her parenting skills.

I spoke with the mother awhile later, when Kate was caught copying someone's homework. Mom was still bitter about "my previous mistake." I once again tried to explain that her daughter was a good person, that I am very fond of her and of my other students, but that I have seen some children not be able to tell their parents about a dangerous situation, and I wouldn't want to see that happen to such a fine person.

Her mother smugly told me "No worries, I told her that she could always tell me anything, she could always call me to come get her, no problem."

Unfortunately her daughter's experience of trying to tell her mother an unpleasant truth does not match the parent's illusion that she has taken care of this problem.

What do you think? Which girl, "Jen" or "Kate," would most likely reach out to her parent?

(The evening after I wrote these words, I read an article in my local paper about a boy receiving his **second** ticket for driving violations. According to the article, he felt he just could not go home and tell his parents; instead he committed suicide.)

Now let's take this one step further. Both girls go on to high school and apply to colleges.

"Jen" has learned to take the lower grade rather than cheat. "Kate" still cheats as a strategy for getting good grades. They both are applying to colleges that use the Common Application. For a list of colleges that use the Common Application, go to Appendix Six, page 87.

Look at the Teacher Evaluation form from the Common Application on the next page. Which student "Jen" or "Kate" will merit the higher score for "integrity"?

Time and again I have heard parents and seniors moan about who got into the preferred school. Parents tell me that their child had higher class rank and scores, but someone else was admitted. The parents assume that the other student had some kind of connection.

Maybe, or maybe not! Back in the 90s, the local bank agreed to abide by my decision, as the class advisor, among three girls ranked first, second, and third in their class to receive a $10,000 a year scholarship for college.

I recommended the girl ranked number three because I had never caught her cheating, she never came in late to class on the day a project was due, and she took the hardest classes. The other two had both cheated in my class as sophomores.

Below is the Common Application's Teacher Evaluation.

Ratings Compared to other students in his or her class year, how do you rate this student in terms of:

No basis		Below average	Average	Good (above average)	Very good (well above average)	Excellent (top 10%)	Outstanding (top 5%)	One of the top few I've encountered (top 1%)
	Academic achievement							
	Intellectual promise							
	Quality of writing							
	Creative, original thought							
	Productive class discussion							
	Respect accorded by faculty							
	Disciplined work habits							
	Maturity							
	Motivation							
	Integrity							
	Concern for others							
	Self-confidence							
	Initiative, independence							
	OVERALL							

Evaluation Please write whatever you think is important about this student, including a description of academic and personal characteristics, as demonstrated in your classroom. We welcome information that will help us to differentiate this student from others. (Feel free to attach an additional sheet or another reference you may have prepared on behalf of this student.)

©

2009 The Common Application, Inc. Reprinted with permission.

For the purposes of clarity, I will use an abbreviated version in future references.

	Good (above average)	Very good (well above average)	Excellent (top 10%)	Outstanding (top 5%)	One of the top few I've encountered (top 1%)
Academic achievement					
Intellectual promise					
Quality of writing					
Creative, original thought					
Productive class discussion					
Respect accorded by faculty					
Disciplined work habits					
Maturity					
Motivation					
Leadership					
Integrity					
Reaction to setbacks					
Concern for others					
Self-confidence					
Initiative, independence					
OVERALL					

Why is integrity so important that the colleges want the teachers to evaluate the applicant?

With technology, cheating is on the rise. As one student told me three years ago, "I wasn't cheating during the test, just asking my friend for help on the test." This perception of cheating is a problem for your child while attending college.

Unlike public high school, some colleges expel students for cheating. The University of Georgia, the University of Virginia, Central Connecticut State University, and Duke, to name a few, have expelled students in recent years for cheating.

Search the Internet for students using their cell phones to cheat, for students buying completed term papers, and for students expelled for sharing answers on Facebook. You will learn that not only is cheating on the rise, but that parents whose goal was college acceptance at any price may discover how costly it is to retain a lawyer to fight their child's expulsion for cheating.

In 2009, Simon Fraser University in Canada instituted a new grade of "FD" for failed for academic dishonesty. Other universities may follow suit.

If you do not address this issue as it arises, your child may not receive the best teacher evaluation, nor be able to eliminate cheating as a time management tool while in college with disappointing and expensive consequences.

Furthermore, cheating in seventh grade can create problems at home. One student, a boy very active in our school play, in sports, and student government, cheated in my class. He waited all weekend to speak to his mother when his father wasn't around. Finally, late Sunday night, he asked his mom to sign a blank piece of paper for "a handwriting assignment in class." He then filled in the rest of the note from the mother explaining she knew all about the cheating incident. The father saw the paper the next morning and confronted his son, making everyone late for work and school.

The father ruefully observed that the family wouldn't have had to go through this drama impacting their jobs if only their son could have told them the truth. The family then went on to set up reasonable limitations on the son's extra activities. In the pursuit of numerous extracurricular activities for the perfect college application, they had over-looked grades and reality, which brings us to the myth of extracurricular activities.

THE MYTH OF EXTRACURRICULAR ACTIVITIES

How can involvement in extracurricular activities possibly be an undesirable behavior? When it deprives a seventh grader of the time needed to learn good study habits.

If your child is in three different activities every day after school in order to have enough activities for the college application, it is time to get a reality check.

How many activities do you think your child needs for the college application for the first three years of high school including summers?

What kinds of activities should they be? If you are thinking "the more, the merrier," you may be working from the paradigm when you applied to college. Let's look at the Common Application.

Including summer and volunteer activity, over the three years, the Common Application has provided only 7 spaces for extracurricular activities

---

The colleges that I have contacted have told me that they will get their diversity from having students with varied interests—each student does not have to be completely diversified. In fact, they are looking for students who can sustain an interest and take on the role of leadership. Look at the column labeled "Approximate time spent" on the application. Colleges want to know how many hours per week and weeks per year the student has dedicated to the activity.

In my opinion, seventh and eighth grade is the perfect time to try different activities with the goal being to find an interest that will sustain your child. You want to show at least one activity that he or she did for all four years of high school and provided leadership and accomplished something.

They should not be doing this at the risk of having to cheat to obtain their grades. You can assure your child that if their grades are a bit lower, they do not show up on the high school transcript for college. This is the time to find balance and sustainable interests.

ACTIVITIES

Extracurricular Please list your **principal** extracurricular, community, volunteer and family activities and hobbies **in the order of their interest to you**. Include specific events and/or major accomplishments such as musical instrument played, varsity letters earned, etc. **To allow us to focus on the highlights of your activities, please complete this section even if you plan to attach a resumé.**

| Grade level or post-graduate (PG) | | | | | Approximate time spent | | When do you participate in the activity? | | Positions held, honors won, or letters earned | If applicable, do you plan to participate in college? |
9	10	11	12	PG	Hours per week	Weeks per year	School year	Summer		
○	○	○	○	○	_____	_____	○	○		○
Activity										
○	○	○	○	○	_____	_____	○	○		○
Activity										
○	○	○	○	○	_____	_____	○	○		○
Activity										
○	○	○	○	○	_____	_____	○	○		○
Activity										
○	○	○	○	○	_____	_____	○	○		○
Activity										
○	○	○	○	○	_____	_____	○	○		○
Activity										
○	○	○	○	○	_____	_____	○	○		○
Activity										

Work Experience Please list **paid** jobs you have held during the past three years (including summer employment).

Specific nature of work	Employer	School year	Summer	Approximate dates (mm/yyyy - mm/yyyy)	Hours per week

Depending on the school your child is in, students with low As and Bs can stay in their honors classes. Ask your school about their honors policies. Many schools believe that any child can try an honors class and then drop down to a regular class. The one exception is in math where the honors class is usually a completely different curriculum than the regular class.

Does this mean I am minimizing the importance of your child's grades? Yes, and no!

The focus on *grades* will not prepare your child for high school; instead focus on *good habits and learning*.

GOOD GRADES VERSUS DISCIPLINED WORK HABITS

Some students had a fairly easy time in elementary school, learning by listening, completing one project at a time, and having one teacher remind students what they need to bring home each afternoon for homework. In elementary school, if a student is absent, work can made up during recess.

When this student reaches seventh grade, he or she struggles with taking on the responsibility of making up work when absent as it is not built into the school day. He or she has to stay up all night to focus on one test or one project and to make sure enough work is done to get the "90" which shows up as an A, indiscernible from a "99" on the report card, in most seventh grades.

But this student and his or her parents squander their student's seventh and eighth grade experience. The student doesn't develop the habits that will sustain him or her when the course work invariably becomes more rigorous in high school and the grades count on the transcript for college.

Most seventh graders understand that they need to do a written assignment.

Wait, I take that back.

Parents frequently make the mistake of asking their seventh grader, "Do you have any homework tonight?" This is an abstract concept. Since many students do not fine-tune their abstract thinking until around age 15, you need to make it concrete for them.

You need to go through each subject with your child i.e., "What do you have for math homework? English? Social studies? Science? Spanish? Reading?"

A parent gave me another example of her child missing an abstract concept. She wasn't going to let her daughter watch a movie if she had homework. She asked her if she had homework, she said "no," pause—"I just have to study for two tests." This student was just focusing on written work to hand in—not connecting to preparing for a test as homework!

If your child only has a class, for example, reading, twice a week, he or she may very well think back on the day, "no reading today, nope, no homework," only to discover the next day there *is* reading and there *was* homework from three days ago.

Many seventh graders don't grasp the idea of reviewing each major subject five or ten minutes a night if there is no written homework.

If you want to give your child the competitive edge, establish a time each day to go through the most current notes from each class, learn five words a night in the foreign language class, five definitions in science, five facts in social studies and five new vocabulary words in English. This habit will sustain your child through high school more than endless activities.

How important are habits? We baby boomers owe the next generation a big apology for a couple of our beliefs. We thought that high IQ and high self-esteem were the keys to success in academics and in life.

The most recent research indicates that something else, and not family economics, is a better predictor of such success.

Ask yourself—what is a better predictor of academic and life success?

The answer is self-discipline.

Self-discipline outperforms IQ and self-esteem. How do you get self-discipline? Through developing good habits and persevering.

For a list of habits that your seventh grader should begin to acquire between now and ninth grade, and suggestions for motivating your child to take on these habits, go to Appendix One, page 73.

Don't underestimate what happens when students start studying for their driver's test and friends start driving. By establishing the expectation now that even if there isn't written homework, your child will sit and review, your child will most likely be rated on the far right on the Teacher Evaluation for disciplined work habits.

	Good (above average)	Very good (well above average)	Excellent (top 10%)	Outstanding (top 5%)	One of the top few I've encountered (top 1%)
Academic achievement					
Intellectual promise					
Quality of writing					
Creative, original thought					
Productive class discussion					
Respect accorded by faculty					
Disciplined work habits					
Maturity					
Motivation					
Leadership					
Integrity					
Reaction to setbacks					
Concern for others					
Self-confidence					
Initiative, independence					
OVERALL					

REACTION TO SETBACKS

Whenever your children have a setback, you naturally react with compassion and concern to mitigate their discomfit. If possible, you will do whatever you can to fix the problem.

In seventh grade, you certainly will have many opportunities to soothe your child, but you must be judicious in what you attempt to fix. If you can steel yourself to let your child have some natural consequences, your child will learn to manage setbacks.

For example, you are at work when you receive the text that your child forgot his project at home. Previously, when this has happened, you would call one of the grandparents to drop it off at the front-desk receptionist. Then, the receptionist interrupts a teacher's delivery to 30 students to be told to advise Junior to pick up his project. Don't do it!

Let your children get the lower grade for lateness. It won't impact their GPA for college transcripts and it will teach them a valuable lesson. Your child will have probably another 50 projects between seventh and twelfth grade, and has a better chance of remembering them if forced to suffer the embarrassment of not handing in a project. You will hear the moaning, "All that work and I couldn't get an A because I forgot it," but you may be providing an opportunity for growth and maturing that other students don't have. It will be reflected in college interviews and essays.

Also, consider it from the perspective of a teacher. When it comes to awards and special opportunities: are we going to recommend a student whose family interrupts class or one who brings in assignments on time? Some parents tell the receptionist to please call between classes, so as not to disrupt. In-between classes, teachers are monitoring the halls, and not near a phone. Also, the receptionist at a large school has too many requests to wait until the end of class. Some schools limit parents to three "rescues" a year in seventh and two in eighth.

The same for forgetting lunch or lunch money, or a permission slip. If the child can't go on a field trip because for two weeks he or she forgot the slip, then let him or her have a natural consequence. A healthy respect for deadlines will help your child.

However, if your child has an accident, then by all means drop off a new set of clothes.

Another common setback is for a student to earn a grade just a bit shy of the desired grade. Usually a few days before the marking period closes, parents panic that the low grade is going to appear on the report card. The usual response at this point is:

1. Review all missing assignments and ask if they can now be handed in for credit.

2. Ask for extra credit.

3. Ask to change the grade.

CAN MISSING ASSIGNMENTS NOW BE HANDED IN?

From most teachers' perspective, the purpose of doing assignments is to better learn and apply the material. If your child did not do the work at the time, the impact from learning within the context of what is taught is gone. Asking "if a child does it, will there then be points awarded" is all about improving grades and not at all about learning. Most teachers will understandably just say "no."

While I am personally against the aforementioned practice, I might be persuaded if the child shows me all of the missing work without the promise of credit. At any rate, it teaches your child that he or she is going to do all of the assignments, even if no credit is earned, so it may as well be done on time for credit.

If the grades are online, parents making this request at the end of the marking period have not been adequately managing their child's work. See page 50 about online grade management.

IS THERE EXTRA CREDIT?

Often parents will tell their children to ask me for extra credit. I tell them that I always give extra credit but never "instead-of-credit." "Instead-of-credit" means you missed homework, missed projects, and didn't prepare adequately for tests and now want to do something else instead of having done homework, completed projects, and studied for tests.

"Instead-of-credit" masks the underlying problem that led to the lower grade in the first place. Masking the problem prevents it from being addressed and corrected before ninth grade. Many teachers share my experience of being a new teacher and offering extra credit to help students who didn't hand in homework. During the first day or two of the new marking period, before final grades are due for the previous marking period, the students miss homework for the new term because they are so busy doing the extra credit for the previous term!

I forgot the home-work again, but I made a cake in the shape of a civil war cannon I still get credit, right?

CAN THE GRADE BE CHANGED?

Some parents try to bully teachers to change grades. They tell teachers, "If you don't change this grade, my child won't get into honors/into the best college/get the best job/ have the best life and it will all be your fault."

MY CHILD'S DESTINY IF YOU CHANGE THIS GRADE

MY CHILD'S DESTINY IF YOU DON'T CHANGE THIS GRADE

Do not make this request. It is an illusion born of parental fear and lack of current information about college acceptances.

Most colleges are interested in how students overcome adversity, and having the parents bully the teachers is not one of the preferred responses. If you can problem-solve what the student needs to do to improve, and then he or she does improve, this could become the basis for a powerful "overcoming adversity" essay.

Look at the example of the Teacher's Evaluation for the Common Application. How will teachers rate your child in the category "overcoming setbacks" in high school if your child does nothing to correct the mistakes that led to the low grades in seventh grade? You owe it to your child's future to learn from this mistake, rather than sweep it under the rug.

Why do you think colleges are interested in this category?

Many college admission officers have confirmed that colleges are interested in their freshmen retention rate and in the quality of campus life.

They do not want students unaccustomed to setbacks on their campus because it contributes to students' suicides. Cornell University is training professors to help students put academic rigor in proper perspective to offset the six suicides in the past academic year.

40 REACTION TO SETBACKS

Where do you want your child to have his or her first setback? In school, surrounded by students drinking or at home, surrounded by grounded adults? Help your child to handle academic setbacks by analyzing and correcting the problem in seventh grade; you'll be glad you did.

	Good (above average)	Very good (well above average)	Excellent (top 10%)	Outstanding (top 5%)	One of the top few I've encountered (top 1%)
Academic achievement					
Intellectual promise					
Quality of writing					
Creative, original thought					
Productive class discussion					
Respect accorded by faculty					
Disciplined work habits					
Maturity					
Motivation					
Leadership					
Integrity					
Reaction to setbacks					
Concern for others					
Self-confidence					
Initiative, independence					
OVERALL					

INITIATIVE AND INDEPENDENCE

On the Teacher Evaluation for the Common Application your child will be rated for initiative and independence. How do you strike the right balance between keeping your child safe while taking steps to be independent?

Universally, seventh-grade teachers want parents to resist the temptation to tell the child, "You are in the big leagues now, let's see how you do and if you can't manage it then we will step in and help."

While for some students this may work, most students need parents to actively teach them how to break simultaneous projects down in to little tasks and complete those tasks long before the deadline. Only a small percentage can innately do this. Students need parents to actively teach them how to manage their time and live a balanced life. The best gift you can give your child is the gift of keeping a planner. You need to motivate your child to:

- ♥ Write down all assignments.

- ♥ Write down all extracurricular activities and appointments.

- ♥ Break a project into small tasks and assign dates to complete each task.

♥ Write down tests and quizzes and assign ten minutes a night to prepare for them in advance of actual test dates.

Today, few students and parents worry about writing down the assignments as they and all assessments are now available online. However, this is creating a dependency on the teacher's remembering to post it, and on the home computer being problem-free. It delays independence and creates a future high-maintenance employee who can't independently work.

How do you motivate your child to do this every day until it becomes a habit? Make it a daily condition for receiving valued electronic time. If your child presents the daily planner with everything recorded, then he or she earns 30 minutes of playing video games or using the computer for social networking, after homework is completed. The parent can check it against the assignments posted online.

Another important step to being independent is the ability to wake up and appropriately groom. If your child is not up, washed, dressed, and able to grab something to eat by a certain departure time, then he or she can not take the cell phone or iPod to school. While many parents flinch at denying themselves their safety line to their child, it will help him or her in the long run. Do it.

With independence comes accountability: students are accountable for work missed while absent. Unlike elementary school, the teachers are not going to approach the student about missed work; it is up to the student to approach the teacher at the appropriate time. Actively teaching your child how to do this will create true self-confidence.

	Good (above average)	Very good (well above average)	Excellent (top 10%)	Outstanding (top 5%)	One of the top few I've encountered (top 1%)
Academic achievement					
Intellectual promise					
Quality of writing					
Creative, original thought					
Productive class discussion					
Respect accorded by faculty					
Disciplined work habits					
Maturity					
Motivation					
Leadership					
Integrity					
Reaction to setbacks					
Concern for others					
Self-confidence					
Initiative, independence					
OVERALL					

SELF-CONFIDENCE

On the Teacher Evaluation for the Common Application your child will be rated for self-confidence. In my opinion, true self-confidence in the classroom comes from trying one's best academically, from exploring new and appropriate activities just for fun, and from learning how to act appropriately even when one makes a mistake.

Many parents make the mistake of trying to build a student's self-esteem by constantly telling him or her they are smart. Recent research indicates it actually leads to non-performance.

For example, two similar groups of students were given a puzzle to solve. When they had solved it, one group was praised for being smart; the other group was praised for working well together and not giving up. When offered another, more challenging puzzle to do, the group praised for being smart refused and the other group eagerly took on the challenge.

I see this in students who are only interested in doing what is easy for them. It is as if a part of them doesn't want to try something hard and discover that they aren't as smart as their parents tell them—it would be an act of disloyalty towards their parents.

In my opinion, being told they are smart leaves students feeling powerless because they did nothing to *be* smart, and therefore they can't do anything to *stay* smart. In my experience, self-confidence comes from persevering and surviving the experience of trying outside the zone of immediate competency. Look to praise your children for actual instances of persevering and working with others, and I believe you will see their true self-confidence increase.

Class Choices

To help your children build self-confidence, let them choose the world language that they want and not the one you want them to take. Ditto for electives.

Also be careful of what you say about learning a language – some parents tell their children that they had four years of a language and can't speak a word of it even though they also had other subjects that they don't use and can't retrieve from their memory banks.

With technology, you are going to be impressed with how much access your child will have to using and maintaining the language! If you tell your children about your own shortcomings in an attempt to bolster their confidence, it sometimes leads to a conflict that the children have to choose between surpassing the parent or repeating the parent's experience. Don't do it; it doesn't help.

Correcting Teacher Errors

You can also help children to build self-confidence by practicing with them how to approach a teacher about missed work and how to inquire politely about an assignment recorded incorrectly. Practice the appropriate tone and timing of the request. This will lead to a more desirable answer and build your children's confidence in their ability to negotiate appropriately with adults.

For example, while in the middle of presenting a new idea to the whole class, a student will suddenly raise his or her hand and announce, "My mother told me to tell you that you forgot to record credit for the homework I missed a few weeks ago when I was on the field trip but I did show it to you."

Instead of this rude interruption, practice with your child to have a printout of the grades with the date and the item in question highlighted to support the student's request. Advise your student to approach the teacher before class starts or at the end of class with the question, "When would be a good time to discuss a missing homework grade with you?"

We secondary teachers record hundreds of grades each week and do make mistakes. Recently I accident-tally recorded a grade of "6" out of 100 when the student had actually scored a grade of "86." Ask your seventh graders how and when they would rectify the mistake. Listen to them and rehearse. This will build self-confidence.

New Year, New Schedule

Another way to build your children's confidence in the beginning of the school year is to help your child to come up with strategies for when to go to the locker, when to go to the bathroom, and how to sort books and binders into a.m. and p.m. chunks so that the student is not carrying everything all day. Practice how to use a combination lock if this is new to them. See Appendix Four, page 83 and Appendix Five, page 85.

Is your child's school building old? If so, the clocks may be all analog and many students today never quite know what time it is because they can't read analog clocks after half past and they are forbidden from checking their cell phones for the correct time in school. This wasn't necessary in elementary school, but with a bell schedule, students are expected to be more aware of time, and those who do exude more self-confidence.

To build confidence, either encourage your student to wear a digital watch or use the school's bell schedule to practice how many minutes are left in the class, based on the analog clock. (This may seem silly, but after I tell parents this, they frequently report back to me that they were amazed that their child couldn't decipher how many minutes were left in the class and felt constantly helpless around these issues of time.)

This is important because future employers will demand that employees be aware of time and show up on time. Our local hospital uses sensors on their ID badges to track their employees' time.

Seventh graders have a warped sense of time – they fear going to their locker or putting their papers in the correct folder will take more time than it actually does. Encourage them to actually time how long it takes and it will build confidence that they can do things quickly. Also, the number of minutes it actually takes may be distorted if they are also trying to text and listen to their iPods simultaneously.

Speaking of numbers, some students start the school year poorly because the first pages of their textbooks are in Roman numerals and they never quite know them. Help them with this and they will be more confident from day one of the new school year.

Online Grades

Some parents mistakenly believe they can build their child's self-confidence by relying on the child to learn how to use the online grading program. Invariably, parents who boast that their computer-savvy child shows them their grades and that they never have to check it themselves, regret that decision when they realize that their child is selectively sharing information.

Students need for their parents to know how to look beyond the summary page of grade averages and be able to click on the individual subject and read the comments about classroom behavior and other information that teachers are sharing vis-à-vis the online grading program.

It makes them accountable, makes them feel safe and secure, and prevents them from making themselves crazy with fear about what will happen when their parents ultimately discover the truth.

Does your school have two kinds of logins for the online grading program, one for students and one for parents? If so, it is best to keep them separate because many of us teachers add comments under out subject area and when we see that the parents have logged in, we believe the parents have read the comments. Sometimes, however, it is the student logging in as the parents and not the parent. The parents wonder why we never contacted them, while we teachers can see that the parents are checking in every day, and doing nothing about the problem. Only later do we discover it was actually their child checking during computer class!

Become familiar with the teachers' web pages with links. Some teachers upload their grading rubrics and their handouts to their teacher page. If two students misplace the worksheet for homework, and one goes to the web site and prints out a copy while the other doesn't, who do you think will feel more self-confident entering class the next day?

Sometimes online grades undermine students' self-confidence because parents can't wait to discuss the items with the student and opt to immediately e-mail the teacher. Parents should fight this temptation and wait until they can discuss face-to-face the item of concern with the child. It gives the child practice discussing disappointing news, and, once past the unpleasantness, the child will realize that he or she survived and moved on, instilling self-confidence.

Parents used to receive updated progress reports from quarterly reports and interim reports. Now parents can access grades a few times a day if they so desire. (In my experience, some do!) The problem is that sometimes parents have so much information that they focus on grades rather than learning. I once had a student who peppered me with the expressions, "How many points is this worth? Is this for a grade?" When we had a one-on-one talk, he told me that his parents only cared about his grades, and that any ungraded activity that would help him to learn was not valued.

He and his parents never discussed what he was learning, or what book he was reading. As the other students learned to speak Spanish, make connections to cognates in English, and bring in examples of songs and words in Spanish that they found just for fun, their confidence grew while this student appeared to be more anxious and less confident.

When parents engage their children in dialogues about what they are learning, when they ask their child to explain a concept or why something was important historically and not just engage their child in status reports on grades, students believe that what they are learning is important. Therefore, they are important—it builds self-confidence.

New Friends

You and your child may be anxious over the summer about the next year's schedule. Most students are anxious about having a friend at the same lunch, and having friends from elementary school in their classes.

Their self-confidence slips when they feel that none of their friends are in their classes. To offset this, you can help your child to feel confident about making new friends by starting to recognize when they are already good at making new acquaintances.

Verbalize when they play with students on a team and some aren't from their school, or at your place of worship, or while visiting a cousin and playing nicely with his or her friends. This will help your child to feel confident about making new friends. Remind your children that their elementary school friends may take the same bus home, or that they might walk home together. Encourage your children to sign up for the same after-school activity as their friends. Usually there are many activities that do not involve sports or academics.

Also, remind them of the old Girl Scouts song:

"Make new friends,

but keep the old;

one is silver and the other gold."

	Good (above average)	Very good (well above average)	Excellent (top 10%)	Outstanding (top 5%)	One of the top few I've encountered (top 1%)
Academic achievement					
Intellectual promise					
Quality of writing					
Creative, original thought					
Productive class discussion					
Respect accorded by faculty					
Disciplined work habits					
Maturity					
Motivation					
Leadership					
Integrity					
Reaction to setbacks					
Concern for others					
Self-confidence					
Initiative, independence					
OVERALL					

RESPECT ACCORDED FACULTY

When your child is applying to colleges, he or she will need to ask a faculty member to write a Teacher Evaluation that includes a rating for the amount of respect the other faculty members have for your child.

Few faculty members respect students who respond poorly to corrections, lie to avoid a consequence, or treat other students badly.

Respond Poorly to Corrections

Growing up in the 50s, the social contract was that all adults had the obligation to correct all children. We children never took it personally, nor did we challenge the adults' authority. Today, some families personalize the corrections that most teachers perceive as coming under the impersonal social contract of adults correcting children. These families need to depersonalize the corrections.

Adolescents will try out new behaviors, and we adults *are obliged* to respond to them. How the adolescent responds to the correction will partially determine the amount of respect accorded by the faculty.

How do you train your child, now, in seventh grade, to respond gracefully to a correction? Use the A–C–T (Adult-Child-Teenager) system to redirect the child's response. This system depersonalizes their behavior and helps adults to remember to depersonalize their reactions.

POST IT: At home, put the next page on the refrigerator or on a little card, wherever you will see it to remind you how to train your child.

EXPLAIN IT: During a neutral time, explain to your children that a little child and an emerging mature teen reside in each of them. Tell them at some point they may act as a little child, and that you are going to walk over to the poster and point out which tactic they are using and invite them to take a step on the path of becoming a mature teenager. Some days they will, and some days they won't be able to.

UNDERSTAND
  IT: As the adult, I don't take their outburst personally. I understand it is just where they are on their own path to maturity. If they persist, I tell them that they need to take that dialogue inside in order to grow. Frequently, in class, if the student prolongs the episode, other students will chime in, urging the student to stop acting like a little kid or a baby.

Little Children respond to corrections with four tactics:

TACTIC

DENY
"No, I'm not..."
"That's not true."

DIVERT
"So and so is..."
"But yesterday X did..."
"Everyone..."

CHALLENGE
"Why do you always..."
"No other parent..."

THREATEN
"Dad says..."
"I'm never gonna visit you ..."
"I'm telling Protective Services..."

Mature Teenagers take ownership of mistakes.

Mature Teenagers do not have to have the last word.

Mature Teenagers process a conflict internally.

Mature Teenagers respond to corrections with:

RESPONSE

APOLOGIZE
"Sorry."

"My bad."

REFLECT
"That was a mistake. I probably hurt _____ by doing that. I can fix this by _____. I won't make that mistake again."

GROW
"Thanks for caring enough about me to help me improve. This will help me to be a better person and fulfill my destiny."

SITUATION: You check online, or the teacher calls
             you and you discover that your child is
             missing multiple assignments.

DENY   "No, I'm not!"

             "That's not true!" "I did them in study
             hall."

SOLUTION

"OK, I understand that as a parent to a seventh
grader, we will run through four responses until we
resolve this. We are right on target with the first one,
denial. (Take out the little card if necessary.)   It feels
like the little child part of you is reacting by denying,
and to your age group, it probably feels like you
haven't missed that many assignments but in reality
you have and we need to figure out why. If you can't
get past denying, then we need to come back to this
in a little while and until we do, X privilege is off-
limits.

DIVERT   "The teacher loses my work."

              "The teacher doesn't like me."

SOLUTION

"OK, the little child part of you is reacting by diverting,
but I need you to not take the role of the victim.
You're not a victim, nor will pretending it's someone
else's fault help you to figure out how to get the work
done. I need you to take a step towards being a
mature teenager and take responsibility; can you do
that for me today? No, well, perhaps tomorrow will

be better – I know you will get there." We need to come back to this in a little while and until we do, X privilege is off-limits.

CHALLENGE   "Why don't you trust me?

              "All of the other parents know that
              this teacher is a problem but you."

SOLUTION

"OK, the little child part of you is reacting by challenging me, but in order for you to learn how to balance all of these different assignments, we need to focus on what you can do. You are not to challenge my job as your parent and the adult in charge. We need to get you to the point where we can problem-solve why your work isn't being completed and handed in. A good start would be for you to apologize, but we must address this issue. If you can't be part of a dialogue about this then we need to take away X privilege and we'll start again later. Can you do that for me today? No, well, perhaps tomorrow will be better—I have seen many glimpses of you being very mature for your age and I know I will see them again."

THREATEN   "I'm gonna go live with Dad."

              "I'm gonna report you as being a bad
              parent."

SOLUTION

"OK, the little child part of you is reacting by threatening me, and it sounds like you are willing to turn on me rather than deal with this problem. You must be really afraid that you will have to make some changes in order to get your work done – so scary that you will threaten you best source of help. I suspect you will have to give up X in order to get your assignments all done—is that what concerns you?

After all of this repetition, you probably have the solution part memorized. Great! Now memorize the words, deny, divert, challenge, and threaten. Begin to closely observe others; practice labeling reactions in your mind and soon the correct response will fall out of your mouth naturally!

By helping your children to identify their own tactics, they can begin to act as mature teenagers when responding to corrections by teachers. This will go along way in earning their teachers' respect.

Lies

If you want your child to stand out among other of today's students, model and encourage your child to tell the truth and accept the consequences of a mistake graciously. Based on my observations of seventh graders, the new moral code is to lie and never admit a mistake; as I saw on one boy's tee shirt, "If you don't get caught, it isn't wrong!"

For example, the students in French class watch *Au Revoir, Les Enfants*, a movie about students during the Holocaust. There is a scene where the priest confiscates hidden food and asks the group of boys to identify which item belongs to which student. Each student admits to owning the individual item.

When we first started showing this movie in public school, this scene garnered no response from students; they were more concerned about the Jewish students rounded up for the concentration camps. Today's students spend an inordinate amount of time asking why would anyone admit to having a forbidden item? They don't understand why a student would admit to a mistake that will certainly extract a consequence.

Here is a list of lies and statements to avoid responsibility that diminish a teacher's respect for a student:

- ♥ "I didn't know there was homework." (Did you check online, write it down, or call a friend?)

- ♥ "I didn't know how to do it." (Did you ask questions in class when it was assigned? Did you start it so late you couldn't call anyone? Did you check online on the teacher's page for help?)

- ♥ "I got a low grade on the project because the teacher doesn't like me." (Really, did the teacher hand back a rubric? What did it say?)

♥ I had a big project in another class, so I didn't do your homework. (Did you leave the work until the last minute? Why didn't you start the other project sooner?)

♥ I didn't know we were having a test today. (Why not? It has been posted online, and on the board for a week and the other students all know.)

♥ The homework is in my locker, can I show you after lunch? (The student is going to do it at lunch. I've had a student go to her locker, and stay around the corner and write it out, pretending it had been in the locker all along.)

Help your children to accept consequences and not lie to teachers; they will be ranked well in respect accorded by faculty, providing they also show concern for others.

64 RESPECT ACCORDED FACULTY

	Good (above average)	Very good (well above average)	Excellent (top 10%)	Outstanding (top 5%)	One of the top few I've encountered (top 1%)
Academic achievement					
Intellectual promise					
Quality of writing					
Creative, original thought					
Productive class discussion					
Respect accorded by faculty					
Disciplined work habits					
Maturity					
Motivation					
Leadership					
Integrity					
Reaction to setbacks					
Concern for others					
Self-confidence					
Initiative, independence					
OVERALL					

CONCERN FOR OTHERS

At some point in your child's adolescence, you may hear from a teacher, principal, guidance counselor, or parent of another child that your child was mean to another person.

Your first reaction may very well be "No one knows my child like I do, and my child wouldn't ever do such a thing."

It is true that parents know their child best within the context of their home and the activities they orchestrate for their child. It is also true that while they were experts on "Child Jamie," they may need time to understand their new "Adolescent Jamie.'"

According to David Walsh in *Why Do They Act This Way*, new brain growth creates "Adolescent Jamie" who will act out of character. Furthermore, "Adolescent Jamie," in the classroom with 30 other students, may be playing to an audience that the parents don't know.

It is hard for parents to learn some unpleasant information about their child. However, it is even harder down the road when they believe that their child has the perfect transcript for a certain college and don't realize that the teacher doing the evaluation has to rate the child unfavorably in the category 'Concern for others.'

66 CONCERN FOR OTHERS

Many parents are bitter about their child not being accepted when they are to blame: they refused to hear from teachers about the way their child treats others and missed the opportunity to correct the problem. If the inappropriate behavior is addressed now, it will be just a temporary phase. Corrected, it won't derail a child's future.

Many of us teachers are concerned that with students always being plugged in with tweeting, Facebooking, and texting that other people are melding into chronic "white" background noise.

To offset students' indifference to others, many schools now require "community service" hours as a requirement for graduation. But this institutionalized compassion also compartmentalizes doing the right thing for X hours outside of normal day-to-day life.

Some of the behaviors that help teachers to accord respect to students include:

- ♥ Helping other students to understand a concept, not just give them the correct answer.

- ♥ Saying "hi" and giving high-fives to the special education students in the halls.

- ♥ Helping a student with dropped items in the classroom or hall.

- ♥ Seeking out the teacher when no other student is around and reporting other students' bullying behavior so that the teacher can catch it.

- ♥ Offering to distribute papers or collect items the teacher handed out in class.

- ♥ Picking up after themselves, not leaving papers or trash on the floor.

♥ Offering to escort someone to the nurse who isn't feeling well.

Discuss these items with your seventh graders. Ask them what they have seen in the hall that was kind and respectful to other students. Remind your children that doing activities from the above list, and then asking the teacher for extra points or whatever the good behavior reward program is in the building, negates doing the right thing.

	Good (above average)	Very good (well above average)	Excellent (top 10%)	Outstanding (top 5%)	One of the top few I've encountered (top 1%)
Academic achievement					
Intellectual promise					
Quality of writing					
Creative, original thought					
Productive class discussion					
Respect accorded by faculty					
Disciplined work habits					
Maturity					
Motivation					
Leadership					
Integrity					
Reaction to setbacks					
Concern for others					
Self-confidence					
Initiative, independence					
OVERALL					

CONCLUSION

My favorite Brazilian legend is the "Pai Coruja." This "father owl" was enamored with his three new babies. He begged the predator, the hawk, to leave his babies alone. The hawk agreed and asked for a description so that he wouldn't eat this owl's babies. The *pai coruja* described them as beautiful, strong, smart, and bright-eyed. A few days later, the babies were missing and a sparrow told the *pai coruja* that the hawk had eaten them! When the *pai coruja* confronted the hawk, he exclaimed "I didn't know they were yours because they were so ugly, weak, and stupid!"

I love this legend because it warns parents that only by abandoning their illusions about their children can they truly protect them.

My sister, the mother of four, never valued this story whenever I told it. She wondered, "What was wrong with the hawk that it couldn't tell how special the babies were?" Now the story clicked for her because she is the grandmother to seven. She struggles with loyalty to protecting her own children's illusions about their children and loyalty to getting the right help for her grandchildren.

Misguided parents need concerned teachers, friends, and family members to support them and their children on the path of a strong work ethic and on the path where actions and decisions do have consequences. It will positively impact the child's Teacher Evaluation for the Common Application and it will help the children to be responsible adults and employees.

It isn't easy when other parents continue on the path of enabling, but you need to make parenting decisions based on your child graduating college and being successful in a job, just not getting into the desired college.

Be strong. Resist succumbing to illusions because of your fear and because of what other parents are doing. Do the right thing. Our country and our economy need strong parents now more than ever.

Keep fighting the good fight!

Ellen Shrager

APPENDICES

APPENDIX ONE—HABITS STUDENTS NEED

Look at the habits on the following pages. Are there any that your student needs to take on? Please, please, please, don't try all of them at once. But start with the one that would change your student's life the most and stick with it until it becomes a habit.

Taking on too many all at once is a recipe for disaster.

WHAT TO DO
AT THE BEGINNING OF CLASS

1. Is my homework out?
2. Is my binder/folder/book for this class out?
3. Do I have my pencil and pen? Is my pencil sharpened?
4. Do I have my assignment book ready?
5. What is the pre-class/bell ringer activity?

WHAT TO DO
AT THE END OF CLASS

1. Is my homework in the homework folder?
2. Did I copy down the assignment?
3. Did I hand in everything for this class?
4. Did I punch holes/put papers in the right binder/folder?
5. Is my binder/folder/book in my bag?
6. Are my pencils/hole punch/sharpener in their right places?
7. Did I leave anything under my desk or on my chair?
8. Do I have trash to toss?
9. Do I know where I am going next?

AFTERNOON/EVENING HABITS

1. At my locker, which books/binders/ folders/gym stuff do I need?
2. Did I plan my relaxation and homework time?
3. Did I start and finish my homework using a timer?
4. If I don't have written work for a class, did I study my notes?
5. Did I put my homework/books/binders/ folders in my book bag?
6. Did I work 15 minutes on projects not due tomorrow?
7. Did I get papers signed for school and return them to my book bag?
8. Did I replace my tissues and pencils and any other supplies?

AFTERNOON/EVENING HABITS

1. Do I have my clothes laid out for tomorrow?
2. Did I put dirty gym clothes in the laundry and pack new ones?
3. Do I have my sports equipment/after school activity supplies?
4. Do I have my band instrument/books and supplies for the classes that don't meet every day?
5. Do I have my bus badge/student ID/lunch/ lunch money?
6. Is my alarm set? Am I going to bed at a reasonable time?
7. Did I plan for breakfast?

HOW TO DO PROJECTS

1. List tasks to do, e.g., project components.
2. List supplies needed/when to get them.
   a. back-up ink/paper/file storage/Internet;
   b. computer programs compatible with school.
3. Estimate amount of time for each task.
4. On calendar, with adult, assign daily tasks.
5. Follow calendar and check off tasks.
6. Pack it! Bring it to school! Bring it to class!

All of the above lists are designed to fit on laminated business cards. Utilizing the front and back, they fit on three separate cards I call "habit cards." When I introduce students to them, sometimes it is a revelation to students from chaotic homes that others actually automatically have these habits. I urge them to take on one habit at a time until the habit is automatic and then try another. Many report back that this is all they needed and it is working for them.

Sometimes, however, parents tell me they have tried everything to organize their child. Perhaps they have even written out the habits that their child needs. Yet, the child has no inner voice that guides him or her to implement the organization. We need to give this child that inner dialogue.

I tell students that the essence of adolescence is to have a little inner child inside them that never ever wants to stop playing video games, shut off the TV, or stop any pleasurable activity. The thought of stopping feels like the little child will die and never have fun again. I urge them to give their inner child a name and to talk to that little one like this: *"OK, Little Ellie, I know you don't want me to start studying, but it will only be for ten minutes. I will set the timer and when it dings I will be right back. I need to do this so Big Ellen can get good grades, a good job, and have lots of time to indulge you."* By switching back and forth for 10 minutes (or else their age plus 2 minutes), students report back to me that they get over their inertia.

APPENDIX TWO—THE MYTH OF THE HEAVY BACKPACK

The media wrongly blames schools for heavy backpacks!

Students lug heavy backpacks for two reasons:

1) anxiety about being late to class;

2) anxiety about forgetting something.

SOLUTION:

1) To help them with their anxiety about being late, I walk out their schedule, analyzing the best time to go to their locker and timing actual trips to the locker. They are amazed that there is time if they focus and hustle!

2) Some parents insist on one heavy binder so their students won't forget anything. I give students two cloth bags, an AM and a PM, which slip into their school bags, or else hang in their lockers. Each bag is labeled with what books/supplies should be in it. They switch to an AM and a PM binder. In the morning, they divide items brought home into the two bags. In the afternoon, before leaving for home, they take what they need from each bag and leave the bags in their lockers. It works!

3) Parents should go through the book bags with their children nightly if they are unorganized, otherwise weekly.

APPENDIX THREE—DRESS CODE VIOLATIONS

Although today's parents understand the adage "It takes a whole village to raise a child," they may not appreciate the villagers' feedback!

Frequently, it is because sometimes adolescents seek to divide the village. A perfect way for an adolescent to divide the village is via the dress code.

Parents wonder why we teachers are so picky about dress code and teachers wonder how the parent let the girl out of the house in that outfit, or that they don't buy a belt for their son to keep his pants up.

The truth frequently lies in what happens on the way to school. Girls roll up their shorts, tie rubber bands around the shirts, and take off their little sweaters to reveal their spaghetti straps.

Parents, with the picture in their mind of how their child was dressed when she left for school, need to ask the teacher calling with the problem to describe what the child is wearing before reacting to the situation.

From my perspective, the dress code protects the girls from having to dress in sexually provocative clothes in order to fit in. When the dress code is eroded because parents and students loudly protest it is unfair, or because they insist that male teachers enforcing the dress code are sexual predators for noticing, it is a hollow victory.

It is a hollow victory because we adults are abandoning our responsibility to keep the children emotionally safe.

Boys are distracted from paying attention by the barrage of flesh in the classrooms, and girls feel they must wear less and less to fit in. Unknown students may interpret a girl's clothing as a billboard that she is sexually inviting, and be incensed that their attention, comments and touches are unwelcomed in the staircase.

Please gather the parents of your daughters' friends together and make a pact to buy school clothes that protect your daughters from unwanted sexual advances.

While you are at it, why do parents want their children with growing bodies to wear flip-flops to school rather than sturdy shoes? Wearing them all the time can lead to foot trouble. Just google "flip flops and foot damage" and then decide if you really want to spend time at the doctors with your child's joint pain, shin splints and twisted ankles.

More than one accident has occurred at school because students crowd the staircase and step on someone's flip-flop as the foot is raised and separated from the sole. This sends the student flying, banging the mouth and cracking the teeth.

Students wearing flip-flops in class tend to remove them and be barefoot in class, and their feet get dirty quickly.

Many employers consider the flip flop unsafe and ban them from the workplace. Help your child to learn that there are boundaries regarding dress codes at work and that using common sense for school outfits is good practice for later

APPENDIX FOUR—ENTERING A NEW BUILDING SUGGESTIONS

Parents can help their children to smoothly transition to a new school building by attending the school tours and the Open House for parents. Consider:

1. Inquire if a bottle of painkiller can be kept at the health suite for your student if you send in a doctor's note for the occasional cramps or headaches. Inform the nurse of any medical issues.

2. Determine the school protocol for letting teachers know if there is something going on. In some schools you contact the guidance counselor, and some schools you contact the lead teacher.

3. Learn how to use the online grading system, if there is one.

4. Learn where to pick up your child if the nurse is sending him or her home sick.

5. Ditto for the procedures for early dismissal if your child has a dental appointment, for example.

6. Read the handouts that the teachers send home the first day about class rules. If your student is going to lose points for not having a

pencil, send in a good supply to be kept in the locker.

7. Read the student handbook carefully.

8. Procure the room map of the new building and highlight the rooms where your child has classes. Review with your child the locations of the bathrooms, office, locker, nurse, and guidance counselor.

9. Find out the nuances of the late activity buses if your school has them. Some routes may be condensed; make sure your child knows where he or she will be dropped off if the route is different from the first bus and that your child knows how to get home from there even if it is dusk.

10. Inquire about the email listserv at the school and join it. Spend time on the school's web site; there is usually valuable information.

11. Find out if there are opportunities for your child to receive extra tutoring during the school day or after school, and how students go about making up missed quizzes and tests.

APPENDIX FIVE—SUMMER SUGGESTIONS

While summer is definitely the time to relax and renew, it is also the time to begin to equip your children with the "soft skills" that they also need to be successful in school.

1. If your goal is for your children to attend college, then each summer they should be adding skills that will help them to thrive. Consider making this summer be the time that they become responsible for their own laundry or responsible for preparing one meal a week for the family.

2. Look for opportunities for your children to negotiate with other adults, e.g., in restaurants, in stores, at the library, or at the doctor's office. This will help them to be comfortable speaking to teachers and administrators about misunderstandings or problems.

3. If your children play fall sports, use the summer to schedule the check-up with the doctor and fill out the necessary forms for your child to play sports, well before the deadline. Model for them not to leave things until the last minute, an important skill for completing school projects.

4. Adjust your children's "plugged-in time" to summer hours, but still have limits.

5. Unlimited video games and or social networking can be addictive and will make it very hard for them to adjust to a schedule in September.

6. Children need limits on their texting; otherwise they will feel comfortable texting and driving, texting in class, texting and walking into traffic, texting and working. A recent new story illustrated that the passengers in a car all braced themselves for an accident except for the passenger texting, whose phone damaged her vision.

7. Communicate with the parents of your children's friends about these ideas and form a united front about summer boundaries.

8. The first day of school, even if there is no homework, spend time going through the brochures from classes and start the habit of at least a half hour a night reviewing the day's information from each class even if there is no written homework.

APPENDIX SIX—INSTITUTIONS ACCEPTING THE COMMON APPLICATION

Below is the list of institutions currently using the Common Application for the 2010-2011.

You might want to visit their website *www.commonapp.org* for an updated list of institutions and for the other forms students need to submit.

There are many fine colleges on this list. There are also many fine colleges not on this list. If you have a particular college in mind for your child, and the college is not on the list below, you most likely can view the required application forms online. Pay particular attention to:

- the form for the teacher recommendation

- the form for extracurricular activities

- the form for essay topics

- the form for explaining a low grade

1.	Allegheny College	196.	New England College
2.	American University	197.	New School U Lang Col
3.	Amherst College	198.	NY Institute of TecH
4.	Arcadia University	199.	New York University
5.	Assumption College	200.	Newbury College
6.	Augsburg College	201.	Niagara University
7.	Augustana College - I	202.	Nichols College
8.	Augustana College - SD	203.	Northeastern University
9.	Austin College	204.	Northland College
10.	Babson College	205.	Northwestern University
11.	Baldwin-Wallace Coll	206.	Notre Dame r University
12.	Bard College	207.	Oberlin College
13.	Barnard College	208.	Occidental College
14.	Bates College	209.	Oglethorpe University
15.	Belmont University	210.	Ohio Northern U
16.	Beloit College	211.	Ohio Wesleyan U
17.	Bennington College	212.	Oklahoma City U
18.	Bentley University	213.	Pace University
19.	Berry College	214.	Pacific Lutheran University
20.	Birmingham-Southern	215.	Pacific University
21.	Boston College	216.	Pepperdine University
22.	Boston University	217.	Philadelphia University
23.	Bowdoin College	218.	Pitzer College
24.	Bradley University	219.	*Plymouth State University
25.	Brandeis University	220.	Polytechnic Ins of NYU
26.	Brown University	221.	Pomona College
27.	Bryant University	222.	Presbyterian College
28.	Bryn Mawr College	223.	Prescott College
29.	Bucknell University	224.	Princeton University
30.	Burlington College	225.	Providence College
31.	Butler University	226.	Quinnipiac University
32.	Cabrini College	227.	Randolph College
33.	Caltech	228.	Randolph-Macon College
34.	California Lutheran U	229.	Reed College
35.	Canisius College	230.	Regis College
36.	Carleton College	231.	Regis University
37.	Carnegie Mellon U	232.	Rensselaer Polytech Inst
38.	Carroll College (MT)	233.	Rhodes College
39.	Case Western Res	234.	Rice University
40.	Catholic U of America	235.	*Richard Stockton NJ
41.	Cazenovia College	236.	Rider University
42.	Cedar Crest College	237.	Ringling College Art & D
43.	Centenary College of	238.	Ripon College
44.	Centre College	239.	Rochester Institute of
45.	Champlain College	240.	Roger Williams U
46.	Chapman University	241.	Rollins College
47.	Chatham College	242.	Rosemont College
48.	Claremont McKenna	243.	Russell Sage College
49.	Clark University	244.	Sacred Heart University
50.	Clarkson University	245.	Sage College of Albany

51.	Coe College	246.	Saint Anselm College
52.	Colby College	247.	St. Bonaventure U
53.	Colby-Sawyer College	248.	St. Catherine University
54.	Colgate University	249.	St. Edward's University
55.	The College of Idaho	250.	St. Francis University
56.	Colof Mt Saint Vincent	251.	St. John Fisher College
57.	*The College of NJ	252.	Saint Joseph's College
58.	College of New Rochelle	253.	Saint Joseph's University
59.	College of St. Benedict	**254.**	St. John's University (
60.	College of the Atlantic	255.	St. Lawrence University
61.	College of the Holy Cross	256.	Saint Leo University
62.	*Col of William & Mary	257.	Saint Louis University
63.	College of Wooster	258.	Saint Mary's College CA
64.	Colorado College	259.	Saint Mary's College IN
65.	*Colorado State U	260.	Saint Mary's U MN
66.	Columbia College Chi	261.	Saint Michael's College
67.	Concordia College NY	262.	St. Norbert College
68.	Connecticut College	263.	St. Olaf College
69.	Converse College	264.	Saint Peter's College
70.	Cornell College	265.	St. Thomas Aquinas Col
71.	Cornell University	266.	Saint Vincent College
72.	Creighton University	267.	Salem College
73.	Curry College	268.	Salve Regina University
74.	Daemen College	269.	Santa Clara University
75.	Dartmouth College	270.	Sarah Lawrence College
76.	Davidson College	271.	Scripps College
77.	Denison University	272.	Seattle Pacific University
78.	DePauw University	273.	Seattle University
79.	Dickinson College	274.	Seton Hall University
80.	Dominican University	275.	Seton Hill University
81.	Dowling College	276.	Sewanee: The U South
82.	Drake University	277.	Siena College
83.	Drew University	278.	Simmons College
84.	Drexel University	279.	Skidmore College
85.	Duke University	280.	Smith College
86.	Earlham College	281.	Southern Methodist
87.	Eckerd College	282.	Southern New Hampshire
88.	Elizabethtown Coll	283.	Southwestern University
89.	Elmira College	284.	Spelman College
90.	Emerson College	285.	Spring Hill College
91.	Emmanuel College	286.	Stanford University
92.	Emory University	287.	*SUNY Binghamton U
93.	Erskine College	288.	*SUNY Buffalo State
94.	Fairfield University	289.	*SUNY Co at Brockport
95.	Fisk University	290.	*SUNY College at Geneseo
96.	Florida Southern	291.	*SUNY College at Oneonta
97.	Fordham University	**292.**	*SUNY Environmental
98.	Franklin & Marshall	293.	*SUNY Cortland
99.	Franklin Pierce	294.	*SUNY Fredonia
100.	Franklin W. Olin –	295.	*SUNY New Paltz

101.	Furman University	296.	*SUNY Oswego
102.	George Fox University	297.	*SUNY Plattsburgh
103.	George Washington U	298.	*SUNY Purchase College
104.	Gettysburg College	299.	*SUNY Stony Brook U
105.	Gonzaga University	300.	*SUNY University at
106.	Goucher College	301.	*SUNY U at Buffalo
107.	Green Mountain Col	302.	Stetson University
108.	Grinnell College	303.	Stevens Institute of Tech
109.	Guilford College	304.	Stevenson University
110.	Gustavus Adolphus	305.	Stonehill College
111.	Hamilton College	306.	Suffolk University
112.	Hamline University	307.	Susquehanna University
113.	Hampden-Sydney e	308.	Swarthmore College
114.	Hampshire College	309.	Sweet Briar College
115.	Hanover College	310.	Syracuse University
116.	Hartwick College	311.	Texas Christian U
117.	Harvard College	312.	Thiel College
118.	Harvey Mudd College	313.	Thomas College
119.	Haverford College	314.	Transylvania University
120.	Hendrix College	315.	Trinity College
121.	Hillsdale College	316.	Trinity University
122.	Hiram College	317.	Tufts University
123.	Hobart & William Smith	318.	Union College
124.	Hofstra University	319.	University of Chicago
125.	Hollins University	320.	University of Dallas
126.	Hood College	321.	University of Dayton
127.	Hope College	322.	*University of Delaware
128.	Illinois College	323.	University of Denver
129.	Illinois Institute of Tech	324.	University of Findlay
130.	Illinois Wesleyan U	325.	University of Great Falls
131.	Immaculata University	326.	University of LaVerne
132.	Iona College	327.	*University of Maine
133.	Ithaca College	328.	*U of Maine Farmington
134.	John Carroll University	329.	*U of Maine at Machias
135.	Johns Hopkins U	330.	*U of Mary Washington
136.	Juniata College	331.	*U of Mass Amherst
137.	Kalamazoo College	332.	*U of Mass Boston
138.	*Keene State College	333.	*U Mass Dartmouth
139.	Kenyon College	334.	*U Mass Lowell
140.	Keystone College	335.	University of Miami
141.	King's College	336.	U of New England
142.	Knox College	337.	*U of New Hampshire
143.	La Salle University	338.	University of New Haven
144.	Lafayette College	339.	U of Notre Dame
145.	Lake Erie College	340.	U of Pennsylvania
146.	Lake Forest College	341.	University of Portland
147.	Lasell College	342.	U of Puget Sound
148.	Lawrence Tech U	343.	University of Redlands
149.	Lawrence University	344.	*U of Rhode Island
150.	Lees-McRae College	345.	University of Richmond

151.	Lehigh University	346.	University of Rochester
152.	LeMoyne College	347.	University of San Diego
153.	Lesley College	348.	U of San Francisco
154.	Lewis & Clark College	349.	University of Scranton
155.	Linfield College	350.	*U of Southern Maine
156.	List College, Seminary	351.	University of Tampa
157.	Long Island University	352.	University of the Pacific
158.	Loyola Marymount U	353.	University of Tulsa
159.	Loyola University MD	354.	*University of Vermont
160.	Loyola University NO	355.	*University of Virginia
161.	Luther College	356.	Ursinus College
162.	Lycoming College	357.	Utica College
163.	Lynn University	358.	Valparaiso University
164.	Macalester College	359.	Vanderbilt University
165.	Manhattan College	360.	Vassar College
166.	Manhattanville College	361.	Villanova University
167.	Marietta College	362.	Virginia Wesleyan Col
168.	Marist College	363.	Wabash College
169.	Marlboro College	364.	Wagner College
170.	Marquette University	365.	Wake Forest University
171.	Marymount Manhattan	366.	Washington & Jefferson
172.	Maryville U St. Louis	367.	Washington and Lee
173.	Mass College of P&H	368.	Washington College
174.	McDaniel College	369.	Washington U St. Louis
175.	Menlo College	370.	Webster University
176.	Mercyhurst College	371.	Wellesley College
177.	Meredith College	372.	Wells College
178.	Merrimack College	373.	Wentworth Institute
179.	*Miami U (Ohio)	374.	Wesleyan University
180.	Middlebury College	375.	Westminster Col - MO
181.	Mills College	376.	Westminster Col - PA
182.	Millsaps College	377.	Westminster Col - Utah
183.	Moravian College	378.	Wheaton College
184.	Morehouse College	379.	Wheelock College
185.	Mount Holyoke Col	380.	Whitman College
186.	Mount St. Mary's	381.	Whittier College
187.	Muhlenberg College	382.	Willamette University
188.	Naropa University	383.	William Jewell College
189.	Nazareth College	384.	Williams College
190.	*New College of FL	385.	Wilson College
		386.	Wittenberg University
		387.	Wofford College
		388.	Worcester Polytech Insti
		389.	Xavier University
		390.	Yale University

REFERENCES

ACT.org National Collegiate Retention Retrieved June 17,
2010 from: http://www.act.org/research/
policymakers/pdf/retain 2009.pdf

Alsop, Ron (October 21, 2008)The Trophy Kids Grow Up:
How the Millennial Generation Is Shaking Up the
Workplace" WSJ. Retrieved June 17, 2010 from:
http://online.wsj.com/article/SB122455219391652725.
html.

Bronson, Po. (February 12, 2007). How not to talk to your kids.
New York Magazine. Retrieved July 22, 2008 from:
http://nymag.com/news/features/27840/.

Bruns, Jerome. 1992. *They can but they don't: Helping students
overcome work inhibition.* New York: Penguin.

CommonApp.org. Teacher Evaluation. Retrieved May 22,
2010 from: *www.commonapp.org/CommonApp
/docs/downloadforms/Teacher_Evaluation.pdf.*

Duckworth, Angela L. and Seligman, Martin E. P. (2005). Self-
discipline outdoes IQ in predicting academic
performance of adolescents. *Psychological Science 16*
(12), 939–944. Retrieved March 1, 2007 from:
www.blackwell-synergy.com/doi/abs/.

Foss, Kathleen and Lathrop, Ann. 2000. *Student Cheating and
Plagiarism in the Internet Era: A Wake-Up Call.*
Englewood: Libraries Unlimited

NCHEMS Information Center Retention Rate Retrieved June 17,
2008 from: http://www.higheredinfo.org/dbrowser/

index . php?submeasure=223&year=2008&level=
nation&mode=graph&state=0

Rathvon, Natalie. 1996. *The unmotivated child.* New York:
Fireside.

Spiegel, Alix. (February 21, 2008). Old-fashioned play builds
serious skills. NPR. Retrieved July 1, 2008 from:
*www.npr.org/templates/story/story.php?storyId=19212
514.*

Walsh, David. 2004. *Why do they act that way?* New York: Free
Press.

Wolf, Anthony. 1996. *Get out of my life but first could you drive
me and Cheryl to the mall?* New York: LLC

ACKNOWLEDGMENTS

I'd like to thank my friends and family for sharing their journey through parenting with me:

Suzanne and Tom Stone

Dee Sharp and Stan Jones

Anne and Dick Howe

John and Michelle Bernard

Donna Pietropaolo, Patricia and George Bernard

Mary and Art Hull

Holly and Jim Frank

Sue and Marc Gerwertz

Janet and Dave Hurlbrink

Lisa and John Hvidza

Jenna, Jon, Laura and Ben Howe

Abby and Jack Waterstreet

Lee and Tim Ames

Donna and Keith Purkey

Stephanie and Doug Grande

Linda Bradley and Jean Farrell

A special thanks to Katy Lemon of the Common Application, Inc. for facilitating permission to use their forms.

My friend, Barb, spent countless hours reading every page and offering many corrections per page. Her editing skills are amazing and her friendship, priceless. Thanks, Barb.

My sister Anne is able to listen to my stories, help me to process the problems, and refine my responses. She makes me a better teacher, a better colleague, and a better person. For the record, she is right only 99.8% of the time.

Although there are many fingerprints all over this story, I alone am responsible for any errors.

Ellen Shrager

Ellen Shrager has been a community college instructor in Massachusetts and a high school teacher in New Hampshire. She is currently a full-time seventh-grade teacher in Pennsylvania.

Mrs. Shrager frequently is the keynote speaker at state and regional conferences, leads workshops and sessions at national conventions such as ASCD, ASCA, NMSA, and ACTFL, and has presented more than 50 school in-services.

She talks about the top 5 changes in society, how they impact the way students are raised, and the behaviors and skills students bring to the classroom. She inspires teachers to build a bridge between where the children are and where they need to be to function in the classroom.

Mrs. Shrager also talks about the top 5 changes in society that influence some parents to enable their children. She helps teachers to discern parental illusions and engage in dialogues with parents in such a way that the parents support appropriate consequences for their children's behavior and effort.

Ellen understands that parents can't do this in a vacuum. Her wish is to help seventh-grade parents to **unite** to let their children accept natural consequences. She suggests:

♥ Guidance counselors at school sponsor a Parent Education Series to discuss the book and support one another.

- ♥ Parent Teacher Association (PTO, PTA, ATP) sponsor a book club to discuss the book and support one another.

- ♥ Sixth-grade parents form a book club to prepare for seventh grade.

- ♥ Pediatricians and nurse practitioners encourage parents to share this book with the parents of their children's friends.

- ♥ Wellness Directors encourage employees with children in middle school to form a support group to help one another to have their children accept natural consequences.

- ♥ Librarians run a book club to help parents and grandparents encourage natural consequences.

To help start a support group, or to share your experiences, contact Ellen Shrager at seventhgradeguide@comcast.net or visit the website *www.seventhgradeguide.org.*

She is currently working on the third edition of her book, *Teacher Dialogues.* She lives in Newtown Square, Pennsylvania with her husband, Ed.

TO ORDER, OR FOR MORE INFORMATION
ON VOLUME DISCOUNTS, CALL
1 (610) 355-0553
E-MAIL: teachervoicepublishing@comcast.net
P.O. BOX 446   VILLANOVA, PA 19085-0446

TEACHER DIALOGUES	$20
THE INVOLVED PARENT'S GUIDE TO 7TH GRADE	$16
FOUR MINUTES A DAY	$12
STUDENT PERFORMANCE CHART	$3
A-C-T- POSTERS	$3
A-C-T- REMINDER CARD	$1
AFTERNOON HABITS CARD	$1
PROJECT CARD	$1
IN-CLASS HABITS CARD	$1

TOTAL

SHIPPING

MORE BOOKS

BY

TEACHER VOICE PUBLISHING

FOUR MINUTES A DAY

TEACHER DIALOGUES

A SCHOOL GUIDE
TO IDENTIFYING AND NEUTRALIZING
"ENTERTAINMENT BULLYING"

FOUR
MINUTES
A DAY

A PARENT AND TEACHER
SURVIVAL GUIDE FOR VICTIMS OF
"ENTERTAINMENT BULLYING"
IN SCHOOL HALLWAYS

by E. C. Bernard

FOUR MINUTES A DAY

BY E. C. BERNARD

TVP

A BLUEPRINT FOR PROTECTING THE VICTIMS OF BULLYING WITH ADVICE FOR PARENTS, TEACHERS, AND SCHOOL ADMINISTRATORS

"My son has been the target of constant teasing starting from the first day of 7th grade. I can't even tell you how much stress and strain the teasing has placed on our family. We were really at a breaking point emotionally. The FOUR MINUTES A DAY project has literally changed his whole perception of school now and has changed our lives at home. He no longer walks in the door from school crying and hating school. He is actually happy." a mother

"Before this alliance was formed, I thought I would have lost hope. Kids were constantly teasing me ... and I was even considering missing school! Once you stepped in with this program, those problems were vanquished and done with. I feel safer now that I walk with students in the halls. Plus, I am even starting to make new friends. Thanks a ton for starting The FOUR MINUTES A DAY project." a 7th grader

"I realized the little things in life one may do, can make a big difference in someone else's life." a student volunteer

WITH GROUNDBREAKING INSIGHT INTO BULLYING, E.C. BERNARD OFFERS A PROVEN SOLUTION TO BULLIED STUDENTS FEELING ISOLATED AND AFRAID IN SCHOOL HALLWAYS.

ISBN 978-0-9793200-7-1

9 780979 320071

51200

FOUR MINUTES A DAY

BY E. C. BERNARD

TYP

If you want to relieve the misery of a student cruelly tormented in school hallways and staircases, then this book can help you to implement your own "FOUR MINUTES A DAY" project* this week!

The goal is to relieve the victim's suffering. While we aren't able to eliminate "*entertainment bullying*," we are able to immediately change the victim's experience in school by surrounding him with volunteers who give four minutes a day to walk with him, befriend him, and encourage him to ignore the bullies. When lovingly and thoroughly implemented, the project can improve the victim's life; his daily angst will be greatly reduced.

When I started such a project, two extraordinary evolutions took place. First, a group of ordinary thirteen-year-old students in a language class evolved into a community of heroes. They and their supportive families deserve all the credit for changing the victim's despair into hope.

Second, many students, including bullies, allowed me to see their world through their eyes. I finally understand why they are motivated to bully and how to stop it. I evolved from a seventh-grade teacher guilty of saying, "It is a cruel age, what can we do?" to a teacher saying, "We must not abdicate our adult responsibilities to victims and bullies just because the problem is complex and difficult." **From my observations, there are two kinds of bullying, "*personal bullying*" and "*entertainment bullying*."**

Third Printing

Teacher Dialogues

by

Ellen Shrager

A Survival Guide to Successful Dialogues with

Low-Performing Students
Indulged Students
Enabling Parents
Cross-Generational Colleagues

Illustrated by Abby Rosley
and Anthony T. Shelton, Sr.

T.V.P.

Dear Colleagues,

As I enter my 25th year of teaching, many changes in society continue to impact my classroom delivery in three ways:

❦ STUDENTS - Five fundamental changes in society influence undesirable behaviors children bring to school. Learn how to build a bridge between where students are and where they need to be in order to function appropriately in the classroom. (See page 59.)

❦ PARENTS - Five different changes in society influence some parents to enable their children. Learn how to listen to enabling parents, discern their illusions, and compassionately offer facts to guide them to support appropriate consequences for their children's behavior and efforts. (See page 117.)

❦ CROSS-GENERATIONAL COLLEAGUES - Similar changes contribute to miscommunication among the cross-generational teaching staff. There are ten implicit rules of conduct that should be made explicit, and can be the springboard for discussion for faculty meetings and for mentor meetings with new teachers. (See page 82)

What we teachers learned in our teacher preparatory courses represent the border of a large jigsaw puzzle — this book will help fill in the missing pieces.

ISBN 978-0-9793200-0-6

Sincerely,
Ellen Shrager